DISCLAIMER

The information contained in this E-Book is for Perspective
and General information purposes only and it should not
be used to make investments of any type. The Author and
Publisher are not Financial advisory and any information
use should not be used for investing.

TABLE OF CONTENTS

INTRODUCTION TO COMMODITIES

In the simplified sense, commodities are things of value produced by different producers, considered as equivalent and uniform in quality in the market. These are items that are grown or produced from land in different parts of the world and traded in the global market. In economics, commodities are a fungible market product used for human convenience. It has no qualitative differentiation across a market. The demand for one type can be different from other type but its price is determined as a function of its market value as a whole.

Generally, commodities are basic resources. It can be classified into 4 types which are as follows.

1. Metals
2. Agriculture
3. Livestock
4. Energy

At a broader level, concerning economic and marketing credentials for differentiations, commodities are divided into two large groups. As the world evolves, the ups and downs of commodity market evolve along with it and so do market preferences. Recognition of economical evolution can help to globally reset resource development and avoid disastrous depletion and economic deflation producing massive detrimental effects on human survival and trade.

Chapter 2

SOFT COMMODITIES TYPES AND HISTORY

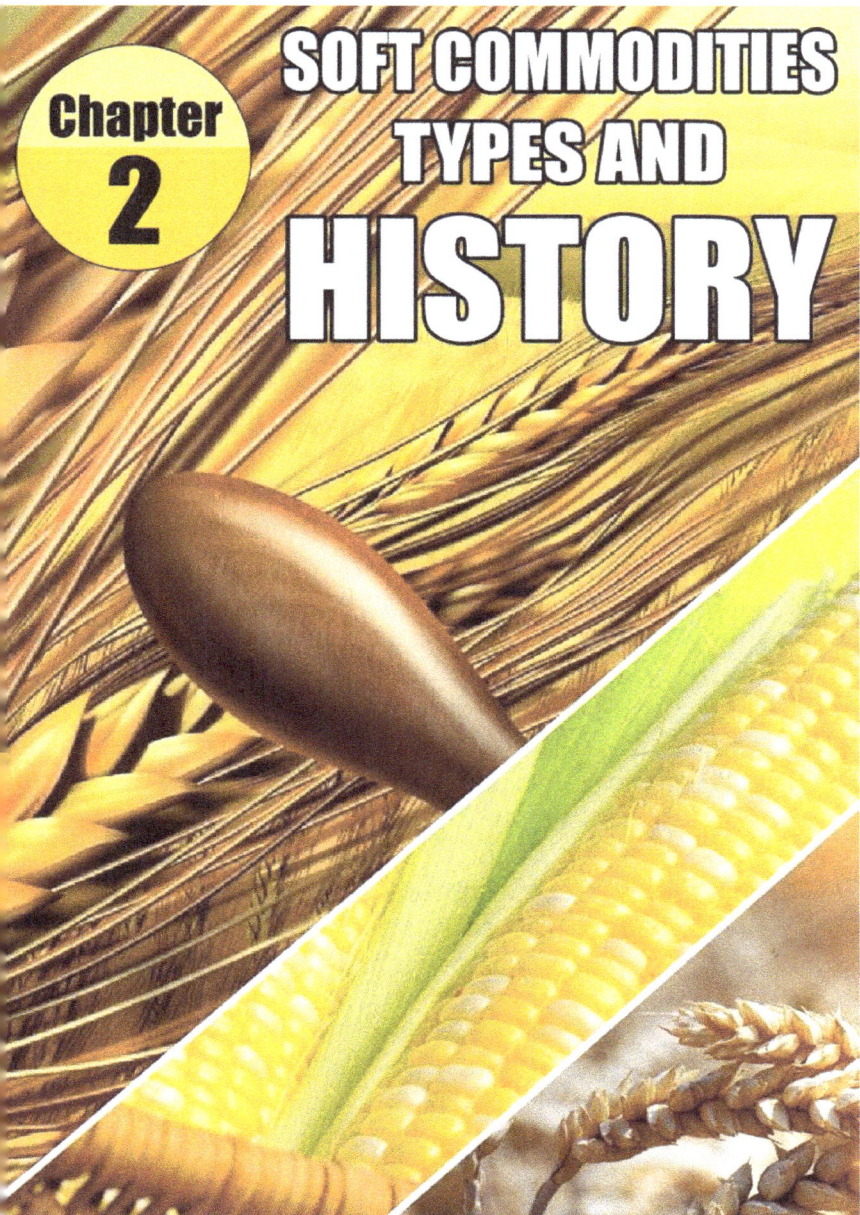

SOFT COMMODITIES TYPES AND HISTORY

Soft commodities are commodities that are grown and not mined like hard commodities. These include coffee, cocoa, soybeans, wheat, sugar, corn, fruit, and livestock. Oil, copper, gold and other minerals and metals are referred as hard commodities. Traders have gradually harmonized various trading contracts to be used in the commodity market. Urbanization demonstrated markets across borders and commodity exchange became a triumphant orator expanding international trade and states handling trading character most effectively developed into dominant marketing centers. Today, internationally traded soft commodities directly or indirectly influence the employment and income of number of people across the globe. Through taxation and redistribution, they make immense contributions to deliver basic services of health and education sector.

SOFT COMMODITIES

&

HARD COMMODITIES

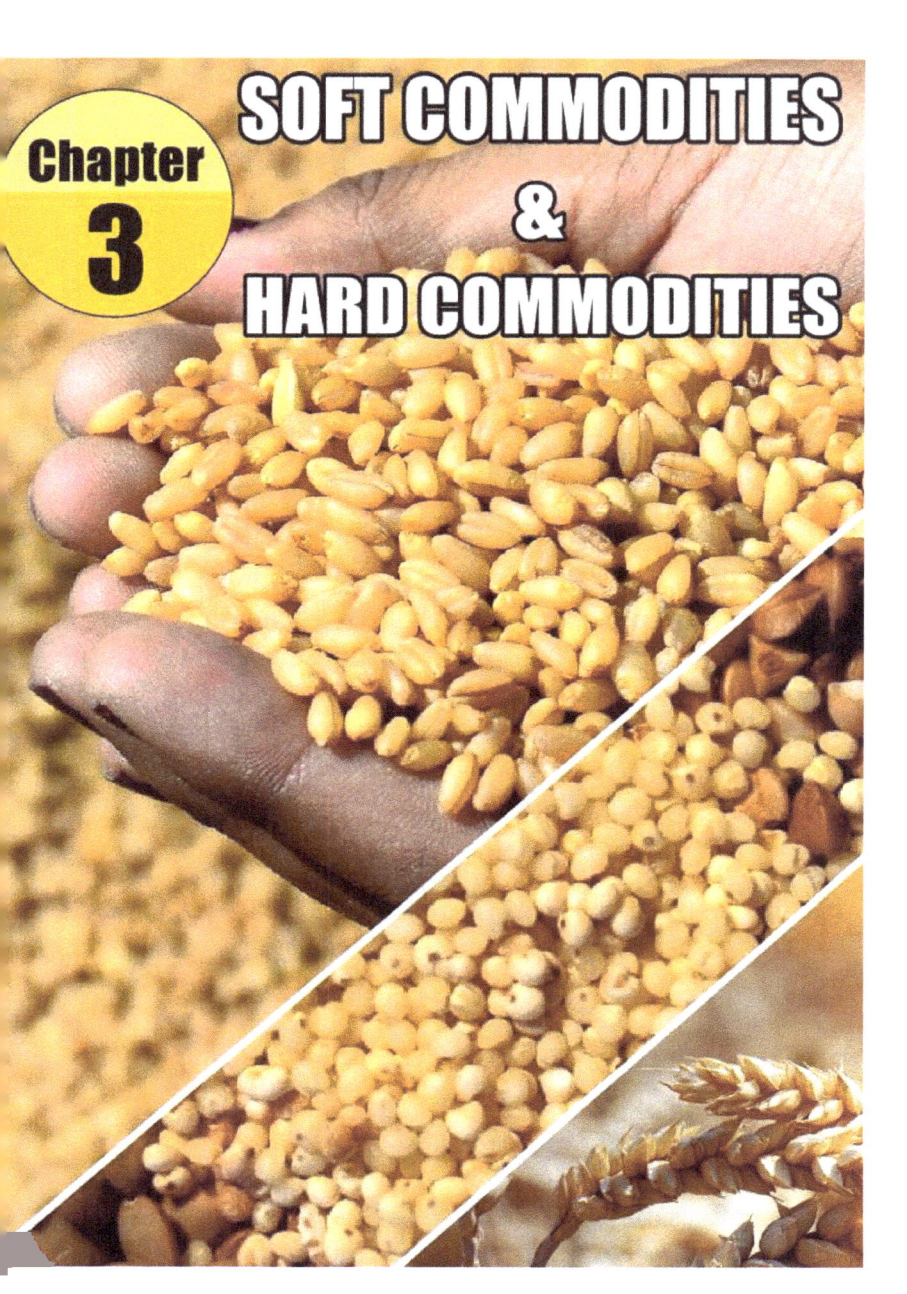

CHAPTER 3

SOFT COMMODITIES & HARD COMMODITIES

Soft commodities include wheat, sugar, cocoa, coffee, soya and orange juice. Hard commodities are mined tangible things such as metals, minerals and oil. Both remain physical assets. The two have differences in terms of economic volatility and rates of return. The six sectors in order of importance are:

1. Crude oil
2. Natural gas
3. Grains
4. Base metals
5. Precious metals
6. Soft commodities
7. Livestock.

These have different fundamentals and price variables. Investors and speculators have preferences based on profits obtained by reaping the gap between the supply-demand periods. Crops included in soft commodities adjust better in times of shortage therefore unable to sustain their prices for long and restrict window for speculative investments.

Hard commodities on the other hand have a wider demand-supply gap thus rendering it a fascination for young a rookie investor. But experienced traders prefer soft commodities as either hedge funds or for long term crisis control because soft commodity has an advantage over hard to avoid bankruptcy suffered in shares. Soft commodities provide the promise of survival in an economic collapse or financial crisis whether local or global level.

Chapter 4

WHY SOFT COMMODITIES are considered a Poor man's Commodity

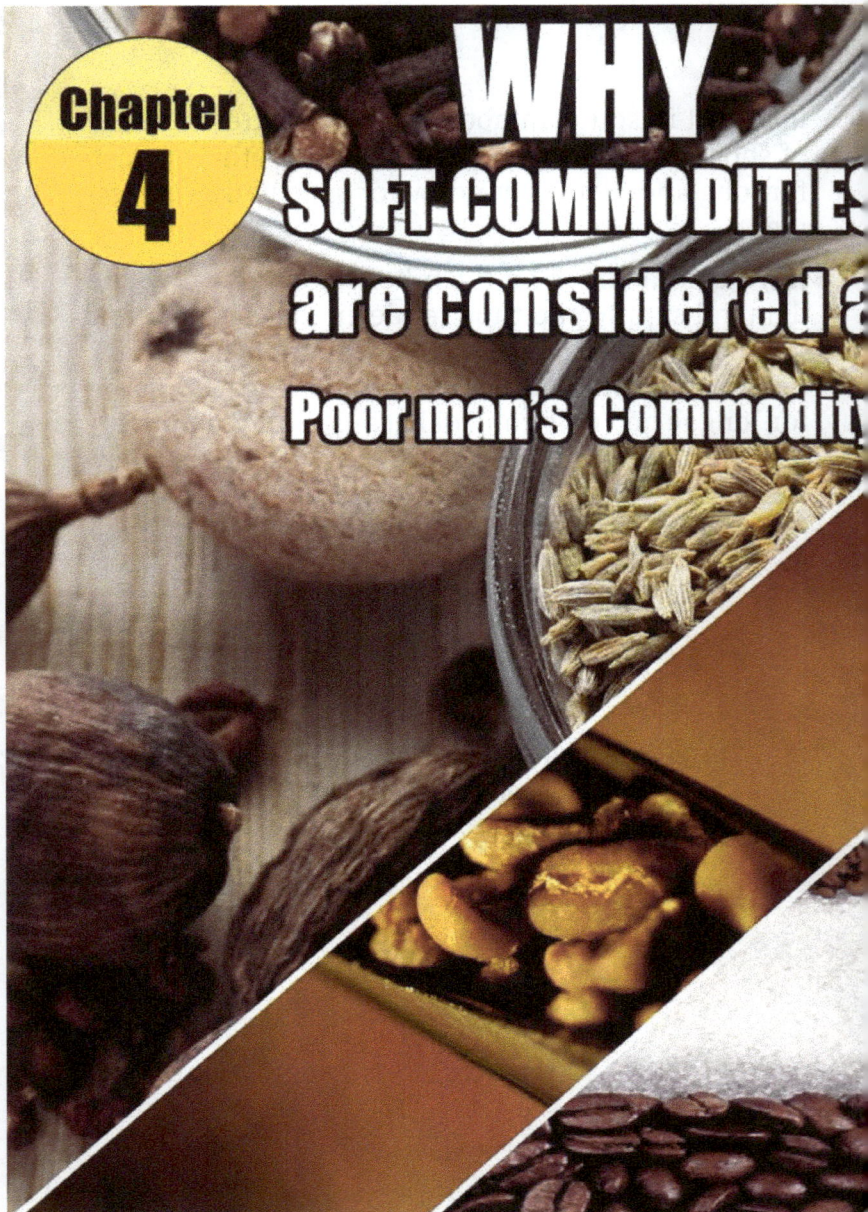

WHY SOFT COMMODITIES ARE CONSIDERED A POOR MAN'S COMMODITY

THE COMMODITY CHAIN

The commodity chain covers a wide range of steps from the primary producer to the refined retail product bought by the consumer in the end. The most initial steps involving the primary producer attain very little percentage of the value added within the chain. In contrast to the hard commodities the raw material purchasing is in the form of bulk trades that yield less profit on big stocks. Weaker bargaining in spot markets, inelastic demands and lack of homogeneity in the modern market, volatility in the economy and dependency on natural calamities render soft commodities a less paid and protected asset to feed with billions. So the billions of the traders and investors are directed at the more alluring hard commodity market that is better paid and protected for in terms of natural disasters and by better laws of inflations and losses, whereas the primary producer of poor soft commodity is at the bottom of the chain and feeding the kings of the trade pyramid. The effect of this discrimination goes beyond the market into the lives of people associated with the specific community. Thus, this dilemma renders poor countries poorer as this has drained their resources and they are unable to get the deserved price.

Standard & Poor's Commodity Index

A commodity price index that measures changes of price in agricultural and industrial commodities is known as Standard & Poor's Commodity Index. It is the best single gauge that tracks a basket of commodities to assess their performance before the investors can enter the future market. Some values fluctuate with their component commodity. Following is an example between 2018 and 2019. Each component is updated and rebalanced annually in the months of January-February.

- Corn ($3.7043-$3.8544)
- Wheat ($4.9757-$4.9414)
- Heating Oil ($2.06-$1.92)
- Crude Oil ($64.90-$57.05)
- Sugar ($0.1225-$0.1235)
- Silver ($15.71-$16.22)
- Copper ($2,533-$2,653)
- Cotton ($0.8212-$0.6737)
- Soybean ($9.3456-$8.9298)
- Coffee ($1.1360-$1.0182)
- Soybean Oil ($0.2993-0$.2932)

Hard commodity as Market royalty

Since the expansion of trade across the world borders, transport has become an integral part of trade itself. The modes of transport gradually evolved to attain faster and efficient means for better product price.

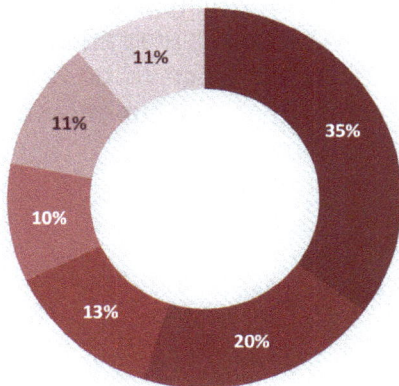

Crude Oil   Heating Oil   Aluminum   Gold   Corn   Wheat

In the modern world, time equals money and traders across the globe wouldn't spare a dime for the time. This has begun the advent of inflation of hard commodities such as oil and aluminum is now increasingly used in transport.

As refined products become increasingly popular in the racing and pacing world so does the machinery required for the refinement of the raw produce. This slow take-over of hard commodities in the modern market clearly declares them as royalty with ever increasing demands and pampered manufacturing.

The war mafia of the world responsible for the provision of weaponry used in the never ending wars all over th world is one of the reasons why a hundred years from now humans will have ample metal bullets but no bread for supper.

The market is in dire need of a democratic rule amongst the commodities to balance the finances and substantially save humanity.

The cyclical trends characterized by long periods of low prices and relatively short periods of high prices constitute the impulsive nature of commodity markets. These trends seem to be influenced by a number of factors that may or may not be in the hands of the mankind.

Risky trading and dependency

Risk in trading if manipulated by human hand can help undertake damage control. Natural calamity is the worst

of punishments in the trading world that largely and mainly affect the soft commodity sector. Pre-assess-ment of this risk unlike others is rarely commenced.

The dependency of soft commodity on the hard commodity is an inevitable resistance towards economic equality. As mentioned earlier the individuality of a single commodity in terms of cost production is over powered by this enslavement. Naturally, the market's supremacy pockets half of the consumer price leaving the soft sector in subordination and thus liable and vulnerable to the entrenched volatility.

Higher taxation

60/40 rule is applied on regulated future contracts. For example, in January 2019, you bought a soft future contract at $50,000. At the end of the year, on December 31, 2019, the market value of the contract increased to $58,000. So 60% ×

$8,000 = $4,800 of your gain is issued to the long-term capital gain tax rate and 40% × $8,000 = $3,200 will be to the Short-term rate. For instance, you sold the contract for $55,000 on March 1, 2020. Since you have already paid the Designated taxes on an $8,000 gain on your 2019 return, your 2019 return will give an account of a loss of $3,000

($58,000 - $55,000), 60% of which is categorized as long-term and 40% of it as short-term.

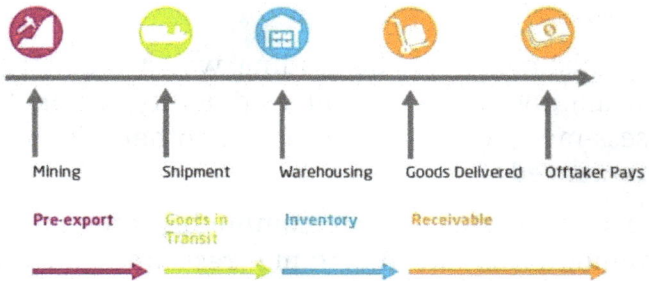

Source: Trade Finance Global. (2019) What is Structured Commodity Finance (SCF)? [Web page] https://www.tradefinanceglobal.com/finance-products/structured-commodity-finance/

Risk Capital

Risk capital consists of investment funds appointed primarily to speculative investments. Risk capital refers to funds used for high-risk, high-reward investments. Such capital will either earn extravagant profits over a specified period of time, or may decline to a portion of the primary amount invested if several endeavors proved unsuccessful, Diversification with hedging investments is the key to successful Investment of risk capital.

Advantages in SOFT COMMODITY Trading

CHAPTER 5

ADVANTAGES IN SOFT COMMODITY TRADING

HEDGED INVESTMENTS:

A hedge is an investment to reduce the risks suffered in case of an unpleasant price movement in an asset. Hedgers use Future contracts to minimize the risk by transferring the price risk to someone with an opposite risk or to a speculator who Is willing to accept risk to make a profit. It works on the same principles as an insurance policy. Soft commodities Demonstrate less liquidation, mimicking an insurance policy of the economic land. Just like insurance, a hedge is never Free but it is the best air bag when our investment suffers a head-on collision, the chances of which although minimal for an experienced investor but do exist. The risk of a hedge fund potentially dropping the profits should never be disregarded but the risk is neutralized by the likelihood of losing it all. One of the many methods of hedging is through derivatives that Include future or forward contracts used in soft commodities. Other methods include diversification.

No default risks

Default risk is when companies or individuals are unable to pay off their debts. Credit ratings are issued to measure the Default risks of a corporation and lenders charge rates of return based on these ratings. Default risk is perhaps one of the Most fundamental types of risk. This is because it ultimately represents the chance that the investor will lose his or her Investment. Bonds issued by the U.S government contrary to the others carry no level of default risk. This is one reason Why corporate bonds will always provide a better position than government bonds.

The time and quantity and price are predator mined so the price movements provide an opportunity for speculators to profit from it. Intercontinental Exchange became the pivot of global trading in soft commodities with its acquirement of the New York Board of Trade in 2007. The exchange now known as ICE Futures U.S. provides futures and options on soft commodities Such as cocoa, sugar, coffee, cotton and orange juice. Few examples of ICE future U.S traded contract specifications are given below.

1. Cocoa

Ivory Coast, Ghana, Indonesia, Brazil, Ecuador and Nigeria grow cocoa & months of delivery are March, May, July and September. For instance, for $1,500/M ton trading on cocoa, the contract has a total value of $15,000. If a trader is trading at $15,000/M ton and a move in market to $1,555/lb. takes place, this is a move of $550. The minimum movement of price is one dollar or $10 per contract.

2. Coffee

Ethiopia is a major producer of coffee. It is delivered in March, May, July, September and December.

3. Cotton

Cotton is used in a wide array of products which makes it one of the most powerful commodities. Months for Cotton is March, May, July and October. Cotton is traded in 50,000-pound contracts.

4. Sugar

Sugar is delivered in March, May, July and October. It is one of the staples used Worldwide and has a dominant commodity index with high weight. If the futures price is $0.1045, the contract has a value of $11,704 ($0.1045/lb x 112,000 pounds = $11,704). If the market moves from $0.1000 to $0.1240, that is equivalent to a dollar move of $2,688.

5. Orange juice

A newcomer in commodity market orange juice concentrates contract equals 15,000 pounds. If the current market price is 90 cents per pound, the contract has a value of $13,500 ($0.90 x 15,000 pounds = $13,500). It is traded in the months of January, March, July, September and December.

Recent Expansions

Population inflation has contributed to the recent expansion in the demand supply ratio and the gap thus created opened gates of ample opportunities for investors to profit in the financial marketplace. The cyclical rise as history suggests might be short term but statistics prove it to be never worthless thus a perfect store for money for the average people.

Image by Gerd Altmann from Pixabay

There are undeniably positive signals for those looking to invest in the soft commodity as this market showcases on consistent and persistent growth rates proved the to be top performers in the past few years. With the emerging climatic changes and global warming, agricultural sector is providing increasingly appealing proposals to the investors market. Tracking is done through ETN (exchange traded notes).

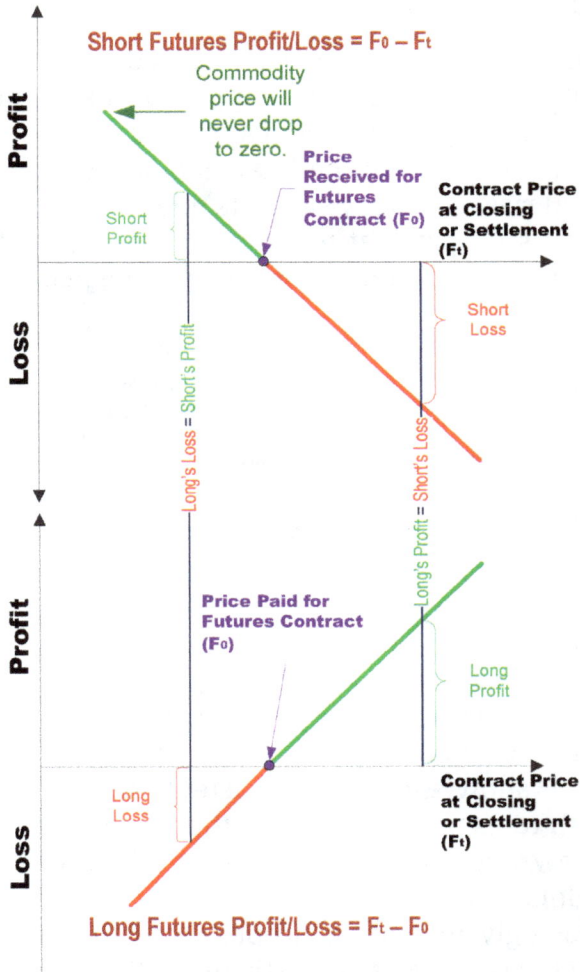

Source: William C. Spaulding. (2019) Futures and Options on Futures.
[Web page] https://thismatter.com/money/futures/futures.html

It is a debt security issued by the bank that is linked
to the performance of a market benchmark. They
resemble equities and index funds and are basi-

cally used for tracking of commodities not owned by them.

Trading in this ETN has been thin, but managed to produce star performers like corn and soya especially in the year 2014. ETN are considered unsecure debts but in reality many of them are backed up by collaterals.

Investors improve basic productivity

The rising demand of higher quantities of agricultural products from China, India and other Asian countries undergoing significant growth and consequently elaborating their economic corridors have augmented investments and subsequently resulted in improving the competency and quality of the produce.

This has also opened giant doors in industrial sector in aiding and taming the aptitude of soft commodity development. Investors provide liquidity in derivative markets and make price discovery more efficient competition and decrease systematic risk in the market. In 2000 Congress passed the Commodity Futures Modernization Act, which gave authorization to the Commodity Futures Trading Commission for five years and revoked an 18-year old ban on trading single stock futures. This redistribution of money made under improved laws introduced to the newbie of the economic world will help reduce the increasing disparity amongst the rich and poor community.

Chapter 6

Soft Commodities a Good Investment in Economic Crisis

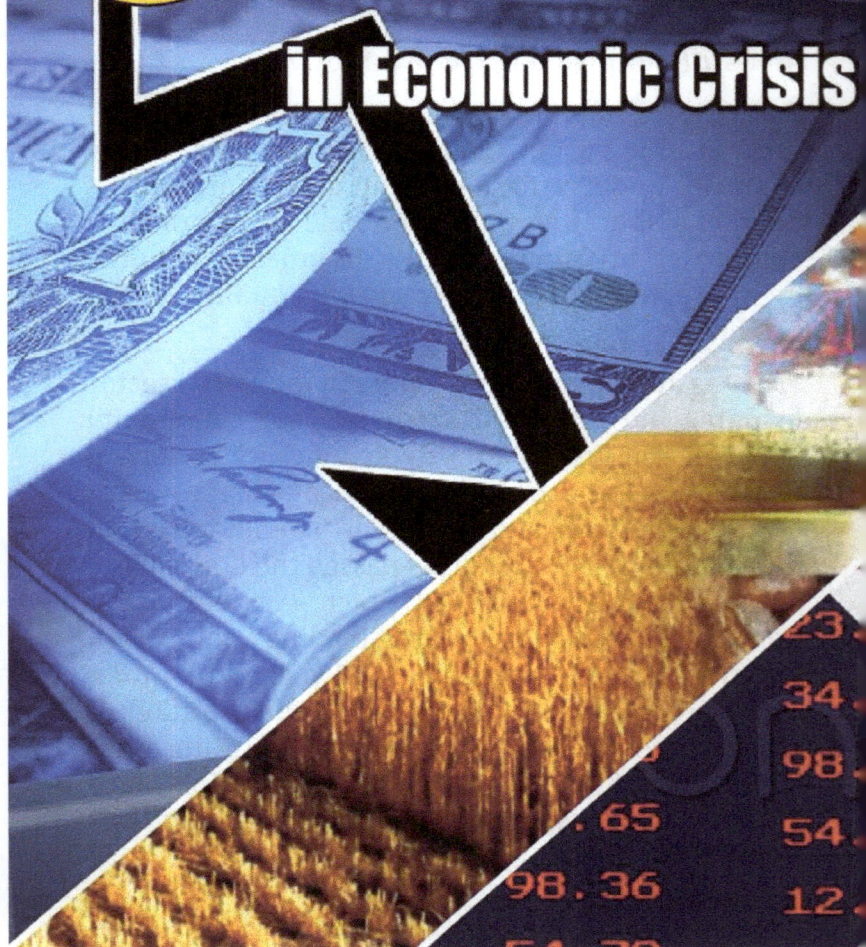

23.
34.
98.
.65
54.
98.36
12

SOFT COMMODITIES A GOOD INVESTMENT IN ECONOMIC CRISIS

A well-diversified portfolio that allocates 5-25% for soft commodity is a reliable armament to combat the economic plunge. Variations in interest rates should allocate the high or low exposure percentage to achieve a profitable trade. With a little valuation, technical and fundamental studies such as tracking mentioned above, effective risk management and volatility strategies help prepare the soft commodities to provide just as good as reserved money in the bank in a state of an economic crunch. A collapse in global market could affect the US. economy by slimming exports and decreasing the revenue of United States multi-national companies. Over the last 5 years, commercial profits have been a stable support for stock prices but that could transform into a disaster if the global economy faces an expanding recession. Soft commodities with their long-term revenue, security from default risk and hedging abilities can well serve as a lifeboat in such stipulation.

STABLE COUNTRIES RELYING ON SOFT COMMODITIES:

The United States of America has a high yield of agriculture relative to other countries. As of 2004:

- Corn average of 160.4 bushels harvested per acre (10.07 t/ha)
- Soybean average of 42.5 bushels harvested per acre (2.86 t/ha)
- Wheat, average of 43.2 bushels harvested per acre.

Stability attained by only hard commodities is a myth believed by many flourish in young and financiers.

Soft commodities give short term variations and are rendered volatile in the market but never go dry as most of the hard commodity corporations do. Also the price of setting up a hard commodity resource plant from scratch is much higher and yields profit in years as compared to soft commodity setups that are low on cost provide quick profits.

This provides better opportunities for average individuals to utilize soft commodity sector for speculations and investments. The opportunity window can yet be widened by organizing the small industry also referred as cottage industries that constitute up to 42% of recently emerging trade giants such as India, following are a list of a few countries yielding from agricultural commodities and boosting their economy on an international scale. These statistics are largely influenced by the size to yield ratio of the producer.

CORN

COUNTRY:	PRODUCTIONS (MT)
United State	366.3
China	257.3
Brazil	94.5

RICE

COUNTRY:	PRODUCTIONS (MT)
China	146.7
India	115.0
Indonesia	36.5

WHEAT

COUNTRY:	PRODUCTIONS (MT)
China	133.5
India	102.1
United State	52.2

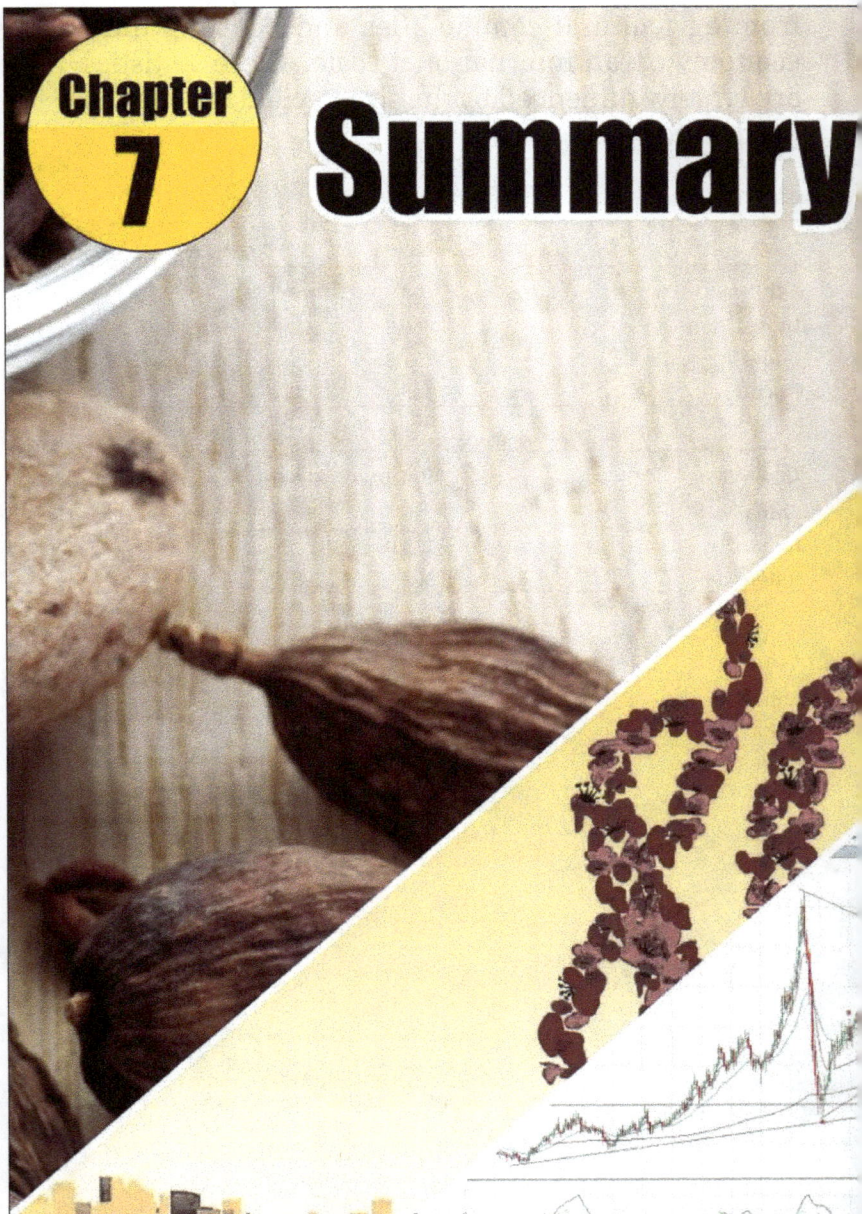

Chapter 7 Summary

SUMMARY

Basic awareness about the availability of commodities is essential for individuals hoping to enter the trading market.

In markets for soft commodities, the commercial market and the users of agricultural products shake hands with investors, in quest of profits from an under-explored asset when there is a rise in inflation or a rapid fall in interest rate. Their existence has both pros and cons.

These pros and cons when developed under strict laws that reduce corruption and imitation and increase transparency will help increase capital and provide better safeguards against market manipu-lations. Strategies that serve economic equality and highlight the greater good as the foremost priority and banish practices that endanger mankind in any part of the world should be actively promoted and implemented.

The main problem is not that the soft commodity is poor; instead the prime fact is that it is an important commodity without which survival would be indefinite. Efforts should be directed at making this sector a secure asset because its sanctuary is directly linked to the refuge of mankind. The need of the hour is for all department of government, industry and investors to address this primary subject in unison and avoid further infection of economic discrimination and greed from tarnishing peace in our world.

ABOUT THE AUTHOR

Carey Harris Lifestyle Entrepreneur and Humanitarian is a person dedicated and focuses more on the life rewards provided to people that enjoy and have a passion for what they are doing. Dedicated to working with People that push Art, Culture and Entertainment forward.